INSIDE MARTIAL ARTS

TAE KWON DO

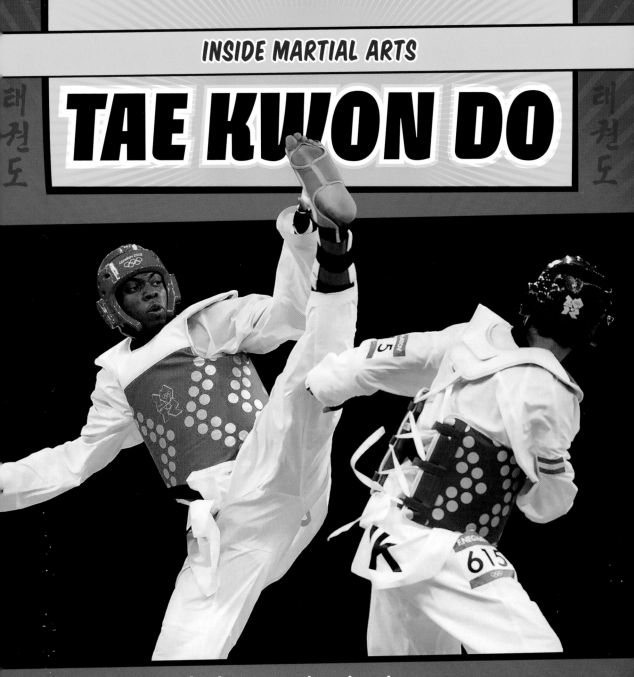

by **Thomas K. and Heather Adamson**

Content Consultant:
Bruce Harris, Chief Executive Officer, USA Taekwondo

SportsZone
An Imprint of Abdo Publishing | www.abdopublishing.com

www.abdopublishing.com

Published by Abdo Publishing, a division of ABDO, PO Box 398166, Minneapolis, Minnesota 55439. Copyright © 2015 by Abdo Consulting Group, Inc. International copyrights reserved in all countries. No part of this book may be reproduced in any form without written permission from the publisher. SportsZone™ is a trademark and logo of Abdo Publishing.

Printed in the United States of America, North Mankato, Minnesota
102014
012015

Cover Photo: Tim Clarke/AP Images
Interior Photos: Tim Clarke/AP Images, 1; Press Association/AP Images, 4–5, 9, 33; Ng Han Guan/AP Images, 7, 19, 22 (top), 23 (top), 23 (bottom), 31, 39, 44; Rob Wilson/Shutterstock Images, 13; Sang Tan/AP Images, 14–15; Sean Kilpatrick, Canadian Press/AP Images, 17; Dmitry Kalinovsky/AP Images, 20; Express Newspapers/AP Images, 22 (bottom); Shutterstock Images, 24–25, 36–37; Melanie Stetson Freeman/The Christian Science Monitor/AP Images, 27; Al Behrman/AP Images, 28–29; Brian Chilson/AP Images, 35; Houston Chronicle, Smiley N. Pool/AP Images, 41; Lee Jin-man/AP Images, 43

Editor: Chrös McDougall
Series Designer: Becky Daum

Library of Congress Control Number: 2014944210

Cataloging-in-Publication Data
Adamson, Thomas K.
  Tae Kwon Do / Thomas K. and Heather Adamson.
    p. cm. – (Inside martial arts)
ISBN 978-1-62403-606-4 (lib. bdg.)
Includes bibliographical references and index.
1. Tae Kwon Do–Juvenile literature.   I. Adamson, Heather. II. Title.
796.815/7–dc23

2014944210

TABLE OF CONTENTS

태권도

태권도

CHAPTER 1

THE HEADHUNTER

Jade Jones is known as "The Headhunter." She's flexible and quick. And she can kick her opponents in the head with lightning speed.

Jones competed in tae kwon do—also known as taekwondo—at the 2012 Olympic Games in London, England. There, she used her high kicks to the head to reach the gold-medal match.

Great Britain's Jade Jones, *right*, kicks China's Hou Yuzhuo during their 2012 Olympic gold-medal bout.

At only 19 years old, Jones was not expected to contend for a medal. Yet she beat the top-ranked athlete in her weight class. With that win, she set herself up to go for gold. To win, she would have to beat defending world champion Hou Yuzhuo of China.

Jones is from Flint, Wales. She competed for the British Olympic team, known as Team GB. So the hometown British fans went wild at the start of the gold-medal match. Jones did not have as much experience as her opponent. But the crowd was on her side. Their support gave her energy and motivation. Jones found a way to focus that energy. She believed she could be a champion.

In the middle of the match, Jones hobbled on the mat. In an earlier Olympic bout, she had injured her foot. Trainers had treated Jones's foot, but it was still sore. The pain flared up as Yuzhuo blocked Jones's kick. Mental toughness is part of tae kwon do training. And Jones did not allow her foot pain to keep her from going for the gold.

Jade Jones is nicknamed "The Headhunter"
for her powerful kicks.

The bout entered its third and final round. Jones landed

several one-point kicks to Yuzhuo's body. One kick was

even hard enough to knock Yuzhuo to the ground. Time was

running out for Yuzhuo. She tried to get into position to

score a four-point spinning kick to the head. Jones knew that

one strike to the head could wipe out her lead in an instant.

So she never let Yuzhuo get into position for such a move. Time ran out. The crowd roared as Jones celebrated her upset win and gold medal.

Jones's famous kicks helped her win an Olympic gold medal. Just as important, however, was her mental discipline. Tae kwon do was still somewhat new to Jones. She had started the martial art at age eight. But she did not begin competition training until age 15. For four years, she trained four or five hours a day. She worked on getting tougher, stronger, and smarter. Her hard work made her an Olympic champion.

Many martial arts are more than physical activities. They are also mental disciplines. Tae kwon do is no exception. It is about more than just the sport. Tae kwon do is a way of being and thinking.

In Korean, the word *tae* means "kick." *Kwon* means "punch." And *do* means "the way." So the entire term *tae kwon do* means "a way of kicking and punching."

**Jade Jones celebrates after winning an
Olympic gold medal in 2012.**

Etiquette and courtesy are important in tae kwon do.
Adults are addressed as "sir" or "ma'am." Everyone treats
one another with respect. Older students are expected
to help younger students. Relationships with others
are important.

TAE KWON DO AND KARATE

Tae kwon do and karate are very similar. They both teach self-defense. They both include kicking and punching. And they both combine physical activity and mental discipline. But tae kwon do has a greater emphasis on kicking. Some say tae kwon do allows for more self-expression, too. Karate focuses more on uniformity. Everyone in class does the movements exactly the same. The biggest difference, though, is that tae kwon do developed in Korea. Karate developed in Japan.

Tae kwon do students are expected to work hard and honestly. For example, the teacher might not be able to watch everyone do push-ups. Knowing this, a student might be tempted to cheat and not touch the chin all the way to the floor on every push-up. But this harms only that student and the team. So tae kwon do students do their best even in the smallest training tasks. In tae kwon do, you do something with full effort or not at all.

Tae kwon do philosophy is to build a better and more

peaceful world. This starts with each person. Tae kwon do strives to make each athlete a better person.

Tae kwon do developed from martial arts around 2,000 years ago in Korea. Japan occupied Korea in 1910. The Japanese outlawed the Korean martial art, which went by many different names. But Korean people secretly handed down the techniques of the art. It actually became more popular during this time. Japan was defeated in World War II in 1945. And tae kwon do traditions were once again allowed in Korea.

KOREAN LANGUAGE

If you study tae kwon do, you will probably learn some Korean, too. Many schools and tournaments use Korean words. The Korean alphabet does not use the same number of letters or sounds as the English alphabet. But it is translated the way it sounds, or phonetically. You will see many different spellings for Korean words. For example, one command is *joon bee*. It means "ready" in English. But the Korean word could be spelled *chung be*, *june bi*, *choonbi*, or any other way that might sound similar.

The martial art continued to rise in popularity. It also became distinguished from its Japanese form, karate.

In the 1960s, tae kwon do began gaining interest in other countries. General Choi Hong Hi became the leader of the International Taekwondo Federation (ITF). He also came up with the name tae kwon do. Over time, the style of tae kwon do became slightly more distinct from karate. Choi believed that tae kwon do is always changing and that it is more effective when it is open to change.

Tae kwon do also quickly became popular as a competition. It became an official Olympic sport in 2000.

Tae kwon do is always changing.

CHAPTER 2

TECHNIQUES AND MOVES

Good moves in tae kwon do begin with the right stance. Stances are the base or starting positions for attacks and defenses. Tae kwon do has many stances. Each has a different usefulness. Picking the right stance leads to success in the sport. For example, a front stance leans forward to deliver a strong punch or a solid block. A back stance turns the body

The proper stance sets up a competitor to effectively attack or defend.

to make it a smaller target for an opponent. A tiger stance requires balance but is the perfect starting point for a quick, fast kick.

Kicks can increase scoring in competition or stop an attacker. It takes practice to make kicks fast and powerful. A front kick gets power from the quick snap at the knee. The ball of the foot hits hard against an opponent's chest or legs. A round kick swings from the hip. It can strike higher on the body. One of the most powerful kicks is a back kick. The turning motion and hard hit of the heel of the foot can knock a person down. Advanced kicks often include jumping and spinning. They can start from a variety of stances.

Tae kwon do also uses powerful punches and hand strikes. A closed hand, or fist, is used for punches. Jabs, hooks, and other styles of punches are used for hitting hard parts of an opponent's body, such as the chest or head. An open hand, or knife hand, can be used to strike soft areas, such as the neck. This chop motion is popular in martial

Slovenia's Franka Anic kicks Canada's Karine Sergerie during a bout at the 2012 Olympic Games.

arts. An elbow smash delivers a hard hit. The bone in the elbow is larger and stronger than finger bones, so it gives a painful wallop. However, not all punches and strikes are allowed in competitions.

Defensive skills are just as useful as strikes. Learning to move away from hits and keep a guard up is important. Good students train to block high moves and low moves from both the inside and outside. Many blocks use a closed fist and the forearm to stop a kick or knock a punch off track. But sometimes a knife hand block is the perfect choice. With the fingers open, a student can block and grab in the same motion for a quick takedown.

Students also learn how to use kicks to stop strikes and move opponents backward. A push kick is a great example. In a push kick, the knee is lifted high and straight before the leg extends in a kick. It can get in the way of an attacker's strikes. It can also deliver a push that moves the attacker away or even knocks the attacker down.

Students practice combinations of offensive and defensive moves by learning forms. A form is a pattern of moves and stances practiced over and over in the same

Athletes must be prepared to defend themselves during a competition.

Two students practice forms.

order. There are no opponents. So practicing forms lets

students show off their proper technique and style. Forms

are also a great way to practice moves without needing

someone to hold or be a target. The forms get longer

and more complicated as students earn higher ranks. Competitions and belt testing have students perform their forms.

Breaking boards is another demonstration skill. It shows the accuracy and power of strikes. Plastic boards are easy to practice with. They can be broken over and over again. With wooden boards, students might start with a 0.5-inch (1.3-cm) board. When that is mastered, they move up. If they keep training, eventually they can break stacks of 1-inch (2.5-cm) boards with creative style.

TAE KWON DO MOVES

태권도 태권도

Stances

Stances form the foundation of tae kwon do. They give competitors a base from which to attack or defend.

Kicks

Competitors can attack and defend with powerful kicks.

Body Positioning

Competitors can avoid attacks by anticipating them and adjusting their bodies to miss the blow.

Hand Strikes

Hand strikes can be used to attack and also to defend in competition.

태
권
도

CHAPTER 3

TRAINING

Tae kwon do training is about discipline. It requires self-control, commitment, and respect. Students take classes or lessons. And boys and girls of different ages might be in the same class. A tae kwon do training space is called a *dojang*. Students bow when entering or leaving the dojang.

Students are grouped into different levels. Different colored belts are used

A teacher works with a student in a dojang.

BELT COLORS

Each school determines the number of belt colors or levels of testing for its students. But belts always work up from white to black. White represents innocence and room to learn and improve. Black is the highest color of belt. It is the opposite of white and represents maturity and knowledge. Students can earn rankings above black. These are usually called degrees, or *dans*.

to represent different skill levels. Black is the highest level of belt. To earn a new belt color, students go through testing. At testing, judges watch students perform their forms and show their moves and stances. Tae kwon do is a sport that trains the mind and body. So some testing includes knowledge and character questions, too. A student who passes testing is given a new belt. The student then moves on to the next level of training.

Tae kwon do requires good conditioning. Students must be strong and flexible. They also need good balance. So they do lots of sit-ups, push-ups, and cardio workouts.

Students practice tae kwon do in a dojang.

Tae kwon do also requires some special gear. Most dojangs have padded floors. They also have punching and kicking bags for practice. In addition, students use stiff padded practice targets. Protective gear, such as helmets and pads, keeps students safe while sparring. Unlike boxing gloves, tae kwon do gloves have open fingers. This allows more movement for blocks and chops.

CHAPTER 4
ADVANCED TAE KWON DO

There is always more to learn in tae kwon do. Advanced students are quicker, stronger, and more flexible than beginning students. They can master more complicated moves. For example, a scissor kick requires jumping high in the air and kicking in a full splits position. It is not a competition sparring kick. But a scissor kick can be used to

Two competitors fly through the air while competing at the 2004 Olympic Games.

take on two attackers. It also creates a great demonstration for breaking two boards at once.

A butterfly kick, or butterfly twist kick, requires acrobatic skills. The spinning and twisting of the body looks much like a gymnast. The kick is not a move designed for competition or self-defense. Rather, it celebrates the art in martial arts. It shows what is possible when the mind and body are in control and focused. It is also the kind of move you see in action movies.

The jumping back kick and the tornado kick are other examples of advanced kicks useful in sparring. They can be hard to defend against and can score points. Learning knee strikes and shin kicks is useful for true combat situations.

Techniques in punching can also advance. Using a hammer fist or a spinning back fist can deliver a powerful strike. Many mixed martial arts fighters take out opponents with these moves.

Spain's Nicolas Garcia Hemme strikes Argentina's Sebastian Eduardo Crismanich with a kick in the 2012 Olympics.

Advanced students must also learn to defend against flying kicks and spinning punches. This requires more training for strength and quickness. Memorizing more complicated and longer forms is one way to train.

Tae kwon do is about more than perfecting movements, though. Part of tae kwon do is understanding the idea that it comes from: Life has balance and possibility.

Koreans use the word *taegeuk* to describe a world of opposites. Their symbol for this is a red swirl and a blue swirl that form one circle. Every move has a counter move. Every opponent can be defeated. The key is to never give up and to never get too confident and stop learning.

Many of the longer forms are named taegeuks in tae kwon do. The name refers to the opposites of offense and defense. Advanced students train their minds to believe in what is possible. If they are defeated, there must also be a way to not be defeated. They do not think, "I can't." They instead try to discover another way.

Students start thinking this way in life, too. If things are not going well, they do not get discouraged. They know they can improve their situation.

A key to tae kwon do is understanding the movements of one's self and one's opponent.

A challenge some tae kwon do schools today offer is weapons training. Students must earn separate ranks for weapons. Weapons training is a great way for students to learn mental and physical coordination. They must understand body movements. Students also must learn

SWORDS

The sword is an ancient weapon. It may not be practical to carry one for self-defense, though. So students instead learn balance, concentration, and coordination through the sword forms. Students practice stances. They also learn forms that show blocking and striking moves. In demonstrations, they can do spins and releases. They can do different drawing and sheathing techniques, too.

how to control and defend against the movement of the weapon. It takes great skill and focus. Students practice attacks and defenses with the weapon.

Tae kwon do has included weapons since ancient times. Early weapons were devised from things people carried with them. Long ago, a long pole was used to carry buckets of water. People also used the pole for self-defense and to protect themselves from wild animals. Poles are still effective weapons. Only slight movements are needed to create powerful motions at the tip of the pole. Students can use the pole to do tricks and aerial moves in demonstrations, too. Swords and nunchuku

are other popular weapons. A nunchuku is two short sticks

connected by a rope or chain.

A young tae kwon do student prepares for a weapons demonstration.

태
권
도

CHAPTER 5
COMPETITIONS

Tae kwon do is traditionally a defensive art. But it is also a sport. Going to competitions and tournaments lets students compare skills. Like games in other sports, competitions keep tae kwon do students motivated. They force the students to be creative, practice respect and sportsmanship, and develop courage. They are also a fun way to meet other students.

Competitions allow athletes of all levels to compare skills.

There are a lot of ways to run tournaments and competitions. Most include some kind of sparring and forms. But tournaments could include board breaking contests, weapons demonstrations, and more. Some events are head-to-head. Others have judges who rate the students individually.

Sparring tournament rules vary. In many settings, the matches consist of three timed rounds. Competitors have two minutes to score as many points as possible. Totals are then added for three rounds. If the score is tied, a fourth round is held.

Tournaments sometimes have different rules about what strikes can be used and how many points the strikes are worth. Olympic scoring, for example, does not allow punches to the head. However, it does credit four points for a spinning kick to the head. The ITF, on the other hand, scores a punch to the head as one point. And it scores a flying kick to the head as three points.

Sparring competitions, such as those at the Olympic
Games, are the most common in tae kwon do.

Points can also be awarded to the opponent for

penalties. *Kyong-go*, or half-point penalties, are warnings.

One point is awarded to the opponent for every two kyong-go

penalties. Holding, grabbing, and pushing the opponent

are examples of these penalties. Attacking below the waist

is another example. Pretending to be hurt or delaying the

match is also not allowed. Other kyong-go penalties include

turning one's back to the opponent to avoid being hit, knee strikes, and kicking the leg or foot on purpose.

Gam-jeom, or full-point penalties, get no warning. These penalties are more serious. Opponents are awarded one point for one of these penalties. Gam-jeom penalties include grabbing the foot in the air to throw down an opponent, attacking after the referee says to stop, and attacking someone who has fallen. Attacking the face on purpose is also a gam-jeom penalty. Extreme disrespect by a competitor or coach will result in one point being awarded to the

THE LOPEZ FAMILY

The Lopez family is the most successful family in competitive tae kwon do. Siblings Steven, Mark, and Diana are all competitors. Their older brother Jean coaches them. Steven has won two Olympic gold medals and five world championships. At the 2008 Olympics, Mark won a silver medal. Steven and Diana each won a bronze medal. It was the first time three siblings had medaled in the same Olympics in any sport.

The Lopez siblings, *from left,* **Mark, Steven, Diana, and Jean, pose before the 2008 Olympic Games. Jean was a coach while his siblings competed in the Games.**

opponent, too. A competitor is disqualified if he or she has four penalties.

Tournaments also sometimes differ in rules about protective gear and how hard players can strike. In the

2012 Olympics, the Protector Scoring System (PSS) had its first major use. The protective pad had sensors built in. And the athletes wore PSS gear to protect themselves and measure hits. The PSS gear registers the force of kicks and punches. This eliminates arguments about whether the judge saw a hit.

A poomsae, or forms competition, requires judges. They rate how well the set patterns are performed. Forms can be done individually or as a team. Sometimes two people will perform their routines at the same time. Then the judges choose one to eliminate.

Weapons demonstrations can also be a judged competition. In American Taekwondo Association contests, students perform routines with their weapons. Judges score their technique and style. They take away points if the weapon is dropped, broken, or held incorrectly.

In addition, tae kwon do is famous for its board breaking competitions. Here, too, there is a lot of variety. There are

A woman breaks a wooden board during a tae kwon do demonstration.

contests for breaking the most boards in a certain amount of time. Other challenges include students breaking thick stacks of boards. This is called power breaking. Some contests also add style to the board breaking. Much like a freestyle event, students earn points for finding creative ways to break the boards.

Generally, students go to tournaments that are in their own organizations. But martial arts also hold a lot of open tournaments. In an open tournament, all different schools can compete. Sometimes these tournaments even feature different types of martial arts. So a tae kwon do student might go up against a karate or judo student.

Tae kwon do and other martial arts continue to gain popularity. Tae kwon do sparring has the honor of being an Olympic competition. It was a demonstration sport only in 1988. That meant medals were not awarded. But it became a full-medal sport in 2000. While tae kwon do will always be a way of defense and discipline, it is also being recognized as a sport. Many young white belts now dream of Olympic gold.

Serbia's Milica Mandic celebrates after winning an Olympic gold medal in 2012.

GLOSSARY

bout
A match or contest.

conditioning
Training to get into good physical shape.

demonstration
Showing how to do something.

discipline
Control over one's own behavior.

form
A pattern of moves and stances for practicing tae kwon do.

maturity
Sensible, responsible behavior.

philosophy
The basic ideas people believe.

self-defense
The act of protecting oneself against attacks.

sensor
Something that can measure changes; sensors inside the PSS measure the force of punches and kicks.

sparring
Fighting with a partner for training or practice; sparring is also what the actual tae kwon do competition fighting is called.

FOR MORE INFORMATION

Further Readings

Haney-Withrow, Anna. *Tae Kwon Do. Martial Arts in Action*. New York: Marshall Cavendish, 2012.

MacKay, Jenny. *Taekwondo. Science Behind Sports*. Farmington Hills, MI: Lucent, 2014.

Wood, Alix. *Tae Kwon Do. A Kid's Guide to Martial Arts*. New York: PowerKids, 2013.

Websites

To learn more about Inside Martial Arts, visit **booklinks.abdopublishing.com**. These links are routinely monitored and updated to provide the most current information available.

INDEX

ABOUT THE AUTHORS

Thomas K. and Heather Adamson have both written lots and lots of nonfiction books for kids. This husband and wife like to work together if they have the chance. When they are not working, the couple likes to take hikes, watch movies, eat pizza, and, of course, read. They live in South Dakota with their two sons.